Strong Defences

Contents

Haydn Middleton

OXFORD

Introduction

You feel safe most of the time, don´t you? You're usually healthy too. You feel pretty well protected. Have you ever wondered *why* you feel that way?

The message of this book is: "You really *are* OK!" Read on and discover what strong defences you have around you.

- Your body has cells that fight germs that can make you sick.
- Like other creatures, your body has adapted so it can defend itself.
- People and animals can find safety in numbers.
- Defences such as walls, gates and security devices help to keep people safe.

Fighting fit

Here's some information from an expert. You know you can trust her: she's a doctor ...

People come to me with their illnesses. They may feel so bad, they think they will never get healthy again. But the human body is very good at sorting itself out.

When the body does need help to get better, doctors step in with medical treatment. Take **viruses**, for instance. They can make you feel *really* unwell. Let's look at how we can defend ourselves against them. There are three ways:

1. Antibodies (see page 4)
2. Immunity (see page 5)
3. Vaccines (see pages 6–7)

Read on to find out more!

A bite from a tick can infect you with **bacteria**. Don't panic! **Antibiotics** can wipe out the bacteria.

1. Antibodies

Viruses are micro-sized invaders that give you colds, flu, mumps, warts and lots of other problems. First the virus invades your body's cells. Then they get your cells to make copies of the virus. In that way the virus starts to multiply.

Your body reacts to protect itself. Your white blood cells make **antibodies**. The antibodies kill the virus or destroy the invaded cells.

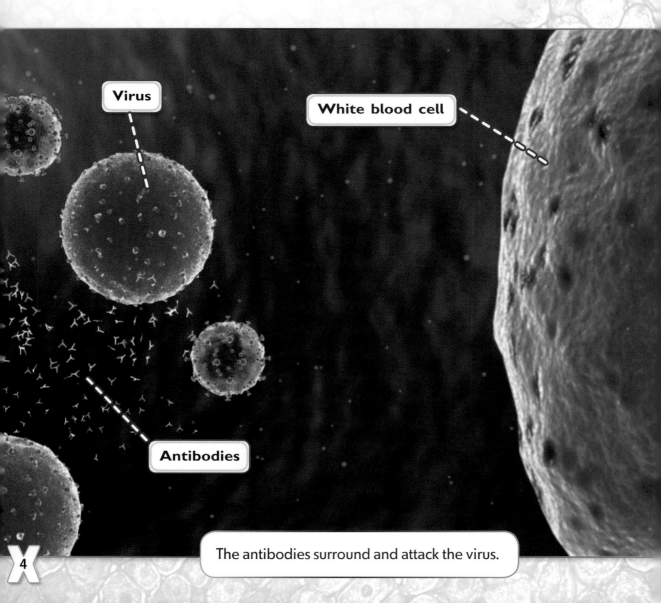

Virus

White blood cell

Antibodies

The antibodies surround and attack the virus.

If someone with a cold sneezes, millions of virus particles spray into the air. That's how a virus spreads.

2. Immunity

Antibodies aren't your only defence against viruses. Some viruses can make you ill only once. That's because after one invasion, your body knows what to expect next time. It recognises the virus and goes all out to zap it *before* it can do real harm.

When a virus can't harm you any more, we say you are **immune** to it.

Over 200 different viruses can give you a cold. You might feel the same each time but it's never quite the same virus.

5

3. Vaccines

Not long ago smallpox was a deadly virus. In 1967, 15 million people around the world got it and 2 million died. But the last case of smallpox was in 1977. It's the first infectious human disease that has been totally wiped out. How?

This little boy has had a disease called polio. Polio used to be common. Now people are vaccinated against it.

Attack as the best form of defence

This may sound odd but for over 200 years doctors have been injecting patients with germs. Not real live ones. Harmless dead germs or bits of them. These **vaccines** make your body *think* it is being invaded by the real thing so it produces antibodies. When you've been given a vaccine, we say you have been vaccinated.

After a vaccination, your white blood cells and antibodies swing into defensive action. The virus can be zapped before you even get sick!

Vaccination stopped smallpox killing millions of people. It also stops young people like you from getting other diseases like measles and mumps.

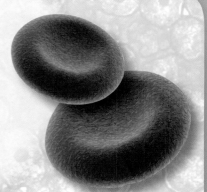

Three childhood diseases (measles, mumps and rubella) are now much less common thanks to a triple MMR vaccination.

Adapt and survive

> Hi, I'm a naturalist. The human body has strong built–in defences. So do lots of birds, animals and plants. They might look fragile but they know how to adapt themselves – and so survive.

> Hummingbirds feed on nectar from flowers.

A stop-start life

The American hummingbird will zoom around happily with its heart beating up to 1260 times a minute. *Your* heart only beats about 90 times a minute. To keep going the hummingbird needs to eat lots of food each day. So when there's no food, like at nights, it goes into a sort of 'frozen' state. Then its heart beats only 50 times a minute. Its breathing slows right down and its temperature drops too. The next day it takes up to an hour to 'thaw out'! That way it can live until it is ten – a ripe old age for a hummingbird!

Alpine snowbells can melt the snow to grow above ground.

Cool plants

You'd think some plants might struggle to survive too. Gentians grow on cold high mountains. They save energy by growing very slowly – putting out just two tiny leaves a year.

Alpine snowbells go underground in winter. Then they send up new shoots in the spring. The heat from these shoots melts the snow above them. Cool!

Castles from the air

Imagine that for 2000 years Martians have been observing our Earth's surface. They might have made this picture report.

Human defences

Humans are friendly, **sociable** creatures. They usually live together in groups. Yet these groups can be very *un*friendly to one another. So many people used to live in **fortified** places.

Two thousand years ago humans lived, worked and played in hill-forts. In times of danger they felt safe inside their defences of high earth walls, wooden fences and ditches.

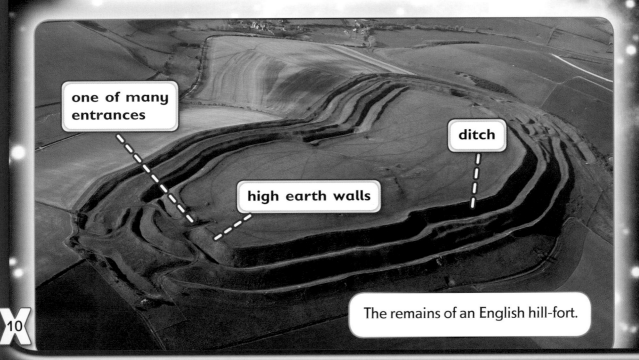

one of many entrances

ditch

high earth walls

The remains of an English hill-fort.

1000 years ago

A thousand years later humans all over Europe started sheltering in castles. Important humans lived in them with their families. So did warriors called knights. Stone castles were hard for other human groups to break into. They would often camp around a castle and cut off its food supplies. This would starve the humans inside until they surrendered. This type of attack was called a **siege**.

100 years ago

By this time the Age of the Castles was over. Humans now used gunpowder and cannons so even the strongest defences could be smashed down. Some top humans still had castles built. Such castles were meant to look pretty, not to stand up to sieges.

Neuschwanstein Castle in Germany – built to look good.

11

Modern defences

Alcatraz Island, off the coast of San Francisco in the USA was once a military fort. Soldiers helped to defend the island from invaders. Then from 1934–1963 it was a prison for criminal humans. First no entry, then no exit! Today human tourists go on holiday trips to this place. Peculiar race!

exercise yard

main cell house

guards' house

boat dock

Aerial view of Alcatraz Island.

The entrance to a gated community in New York City.

Around the start of the twenty-first century, humans all over Earth started living in places *like* castles again. These humans were worried that criminals would burgle their homes. So they set up 'gated communities' in their cities.

A gated community is a bit like an old hill-fort. The group of homes inside is walled off from the rest of the public. Round-the-clock guards and **security** cameras make the resident humans feel even safer.

EXTRA STRONG
KEEP IT SAFE!
DEFENCE SERVICES

Great deals to make your home more secure

Home Intruder Alarm HIA7X Wire Free

Easy to install and operate. ESDS technical support offered 24/7.

Pushbutton Window Locks PBW166

Six out of ten burglars get in through a window. So protect your home with these easy-to-install window locks. Buy ten, get two free! (ESDS also supplies locks for shed and garage windows too. Remember: sheds and garages are full of tools criminals can use to burgle your home.)

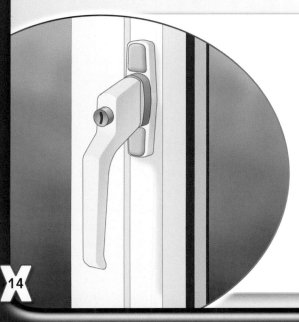

Video Door Entry Kit VDEK2A

When someone calls at your home, can you tell who it is before you open the door? Fit one of our new ESDS video kits. The outside camera films your caller – then displays his or her image on your TV screen!

Smoke Detector SD – 49Z

Do you smell burning? This classic ESDS early-warning bleeper will sniff out any smoke long before you do. Battery operated.

ESDS Fire Safe FS945

Keep your things secure in an ESDS fire safe. Will protect papers for an hour in fires that reach temperatures of 945°C! Electronic locking option available.

Safety in numbers

Hi there! Me again. Let's get back to nature now. People live in communities to make their lives safer. Lots of birds, fish and animals do the same.

Let's stick together

Imagine you're a wildebeest, out on the open plains of Africa. You're all alone. You're always on the lookout for hungry **predators** who might fancy you for dinner. That can get tiring. If you're part of a herd, the other wildebeests can be on the lookout too. If danger appears, they can sound the alarm. Then everyone runs for cover!

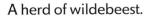

A herd of wildebeest.

It works the other way round too. Some predators like to hunt in packs. It would be tough for a single lion to pick off even the smallest elephant calf. A pack of them gets the job done much more efficiently. For them, it's strength in numbers.

Older elephants surround the young to protect them from attack.

You peck my back – and I'll let you ride on it!

Sometimes different sorts of creatures form communities to make life easier. Birds called oxpeckers have a favourite food: blood. Blood is also the favourite food of tiny pests like ticks and other **parasites**. Oxpeckers get their blood by pecking blood-filled ticks from the backs of big animals like antelopes and zebras.

Oxpeckers on Impalas.

The animals are usually happy to give the oxpeckers a ride. Then they get their own tiny parasites picked off. Also when a predator appears on the horizon, the oxpeckers sound a loud alarm cry.

No relationship is ever 100 per cent perfect, though. Sometimes oxpeckers suck blood straight from the big animal. Now that's *bad* table manners!

These white birds are egrets. They like to hang out near hippos and rhinos. Why? Those beasts are so big, they stir up the ground wherever they walk. That means insects appear for the egrets to eat.

Protecting your patch

Most people feel safer belonging to a nation or country. Big **territories** need strong defences too – from foreign invaders.

Today they're defended by armies, navies and air forces. In the past people also used walls. You can still see bits of these two walls.

Hadrian's Wall

Country: Britain

Date built: Started in the year 122

Length: 117 kilometres

Purpose: To protect Roman Britain from tribes living in what is now Scotland.

Facts: Named after the Roman Emperor Hadrian. Sixteen big forts were built along it, each with 500–1000 Romans inside.

Strange but true: The Romans built the wall to keep out foreign invaders but *they* had invaded Britain from Italy!

Great Wall of China

Country: China

Date built: Started over 2000 years ago, then updated over centuries. Really not just one wall but several linked walls.

Length: About 2700 kilometres – but some say much longer!

Purpose: To protect Chinese border towns and farming villages from roaming tribespeople to the north.

Facts: Some sections are 4.5–9 metres wide and rise as high as 7.5 metres. Made of stone, brick and packed earth, with many watchtowers and barracks.

Strange but UNTRUE: "The Great Wall is the only man-made thing on Earth big enough to be seen from the Moon."

Don't mess with the robin!

It's not only people who defend their territory. The little red-breasted robin has his own patch of territory all year round. He will defend it to the death.

In winter, each robin 'rules' over its own patch. (You could fit about 12 robin patches into a football pitch.) Only the ruling robin has feeding rights here.

A robin singing to mark his territory.

Baby robins have speckled breasts. If they were red, their dads might attack them instead of feeding them!

Male robins defend their territories very fiercely. If another male tries to invade, the local robin puts up a big fight. In some areas, one robin in ten dies in these fights. Getting a territory really is a matter of life and death. If a robin doesn't have one, he will starve.

Red alert!

Male robins are a brighter red than females. If one male spots another on his territory, he'll attack it fiercely! He will even attack stuffed robins or tufts of red feathers.

WHAT IS ONE OF THE BIGGEST THREATS TO OUR SAFETY TODAY?

WAR? DISEASE? POLLUTION? POVERTY? CRIME?

According to the world's top scientists, we've also got to watch out for water. Yes, that's right. Water! We can't live without it. Nor can we live with too much of it.

IN DEEP WATER

We all know about global warming. Water expands as it heats up so if the world gets warmer sea levels could rise. But that's not all. The polar ice caps are melting. If the ice caps continue to melt, sea levels could rise by several metres. Much of our coastline could be lost to the sea.

Places that used to have regular amounts of rain could soon get heavy downpours, like the **monsoon** in south-east Asia.

An iceberg melting.

WHERE ARE THE RISK AREAS?

Areas near rivers and on low-lying coasts are high risk areas for flooding. Such regions – like much of Bangladesh in Asia – *already* get regular floods. This makes the ground great for growing crops so millions of people live and work there. What if future floods are even worse than the great Bangladesh flood of 1998? Ten *million* people had their homes swept away then!

Rowing through flood water in Bangladesh.

BIG CITIES AT HIGH FLOOD RISK

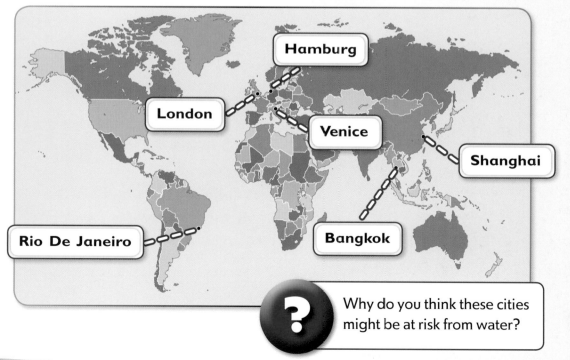

Hamburg

London

Venice

Shanghai

Rio De Janeiro

Bangkok

? Why do you think these cities might be at risk from water?

Don't panic. There are solutions!

DYKES

People have been defending themselves from rising water for centuries. In the Netherlands they build long mounds called **dykes** on both sides of their rivers. These usually hold back water in flood times.

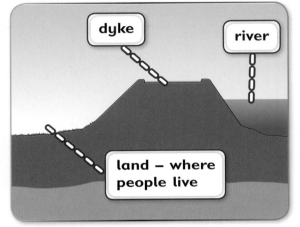

dyke

river

land – where people live

The dykes push back the water from the land. Pumps are built on dykes and used to pump water off the land.

THE THAMES BARRIER

Modern day London is protected by a man-made **barrier**. This is a state-of-the-art system of floodgates across the River Thames. The tides on this river get very high. Each of the barrier's four main gates can be raised to the height of a five-storey building.

one of
ten gates

water is
held back

The barrier prevents the River Thames from flooding London.

Space: the final frontier

One evening in October 1938, shocking news came over the radio in the USA. Earth was being invaded by Martians!

The radio described how aliens had landed. They were launching a deadly poison gas attack on Americans. Listeners panicked. They rushed out of their homes. They hid underground. They got in their cars and tried to drive to safety.

Then the truth came out. It was just a radio play. Actors were performing a radio version of a novel by H.G. Wells called *The War of the Worlds!*

The front cover of the novel, first published in 1898.

Could it really happen?

Germs to the rescue

We still wonder if there's intelligent life elsewhere in the universe. *Then* we wonder if **extraterrestrials** would want to invade Earth. If they did, what defences would we have? It's hard to know until we're under attack!

The Martian invasion in *The War of the Worlds* didn't succeed. Why not? Do you remember those tiny bugs and germs the doctor talked about on pages 3–7? Well, coming from another planet, the Martians had no immunity to Earth's illnesses. So they got sick and died!

Observers in orbit

When the fake Martians invaded in 1938, people didn't know what was 'out there' in space. Today, man-made satellites in space send pictures back to Earth.

- Satellites watch other planets. So if aliens *are* coming to Earth, at least we should know before they land!

- Cameras in space can see the weather. So we can take cover if anything dangerous, like a hurricane, is coming!

- Communications satellites make it easy to share information. Phone-call signals can be sent right across the world via these satellites — as can emails and live TV programmes.

If people can communicate with one another, they're better prepared to take action when danger threatens. Information is strength!

So you see, you really are protected by some very **STRONG DEFENCES!**

This is a **meteorite**. Giant meteorites could be a bigger threat than aliens. Experts think one hit our planet 65 million years ago, wiping out the dinosaurs. How might we defend ourselves against one of these?

Glossary

antibiotics	medicine that kills bacteria
antibody	something your body makes to fight infections
bacteria	tiny living things, some of which cause diseases
barrier	a fence or something that stands in the way
dyke	a barrier built along a river to hold back the water
extraterrestrial	something that does not come from our planet, Earth
fortify	make strong
immune	safe from disease or illness
meteorite	a piece of rock that moves through space
monsoon	a time of very heavy rains
parasite	a plant or animal that lives on another plant or another animal
predator	an animal that hunts and eats other animals
resident	living in a place
security	when something is made safe and firm
siege	a time when an army surrounds a town or castle so that people or things cannot get in or out
sociable	friendly
territory	land that belongs to one person, country or animal
tick	a small insect that bites humans and animals and sucks their blood
vaccine	medicine that protects us against a particular disease
virus	a tiny living thing that can cause diseases

Index